Published by Creative Education and
Creative Paperbacks
P.O. Box 227, Mankato, Minnesota 56002
Creative Education and Creative Paperbacks
are imprints of The Creative Company
www.thecreativecompany.us

Design by The Design Lab
Production by Chelsey Luther
Printed in the United States of America

Photographs by Corbis (Michel Denis-Huot/Hemis),
Dreamstime (Galyna Andrushko, Derek Burke,
Edwardje, Notweston), National Geographic
Creative (KLAUS NIGGE), Shutterstock (Steffen
Foerster, kuponjabah, Fabien Monteil), SuperStock
(Biosphoto, Minden Pictures, NHPA)

Library of Congress Cataloging-in-Publication Data
Riggs, Kate.
Flamingos / Kate Riggs.
p. cm. — (Amazing animals)
Summary: A basic exploration of the appearance,
behavior, and habitat of flamingos, the long-legged
wading birds. Also included is a story from folklore
explaining how flamingos came to live at salt lakes.
Includes index.
ISBN 978-1-60818-488-0 (hardcover)
ISBN 978-1-62832-088-6 (pbk)
1. Flamingos—Juvenile literature. I. Title. II. Series:
Amazing animals.
QL696.C56R54 2015
598.3'5—dc23   2013051248

CCSS: RI.1.1, 2, 4, 5, 6, 7; RI.2.2, 5, 6, 7, 10;
RI.3.1, 5, 7, 8; RF.1.1, 3, 4; RF.2.3, 4

9 8 7 6 5 4 3 2

AMAZING ANIMALS

FLAMINGOS

BY KATE RIGGS

CREATIVE EDUCATION • CREATIVE PAPERBACKS

Flamingos are colorful birds. Old World flamingos live in Africa and parts of Asia and Europe. New World flamingos are found in the Americas. Many flamingos live near **soda lakes**.

soda lakes bodies of water that are very salty and dry up when there is no rain

Flamingos have long legs and long necks. Their feathers are waterproof. They have webbing between their toes. Many flamingos are red, orange, or pink. Andean flamingos have pale pink bodies. But they have yellow legs. Other flamingos have pink or orange legs.

*Webbed feet help
flamingos walk on
sandy and wet ground*

The biggest flamingos weigh up to nine pounds (4 kg). When they stretch out their wings, they can reach 5.5 feet (1.7 m). The smallest flamingos weigh about 3.5 pounds (1.6 kg).

A greater flamingo can be twice the size of lesser flamingos

Flamingos live in hot, watery places. They stomp in the mud when they walk through water that is not very deep. Sometimes they fly across deeper water.

*Flamingos have to
get a running start
before flying*

Carotenoids (keh-RAH-teh-noydz) give flamingos their colors

Flamingos put their heads upside down to feed in water. They use their **bills** to scoop up water. They eat plant seeds, bugs, and tiny creatures found in the water. Flamingos get their colors from the foods they eat.

bills beaks, or the part of a bird's mouth that sticks out from its face

Newborn flamingos are about the size of tennis balls

The male and female flamingo build a nest out of mud. Then a female flamingo lays one egg. The **chick** breaks the egg when it hatches. New chicks have fluffy **down**. They drink a special liquid called crop milk. Young chicks stay together in groups called crèches.

chick a baby flamingo

down the soft feathers of a young bird

African animals called hyenas will chase flamingos in water

Other animals try to take flamingo chicks and eggs. Foxes, other birds, and big cats are some flamingo **predators**. Flamingos live in groups called flocks to keep each other safe.

predators animals that kill and eat other animals

Flamingos honk and make other sounds to talk to each other

Flocks sometimes come together to form **colonies**. Thousands of flamingos look for food together. They march or dance across the water. Then they look for mates.

colonies groups of flamingo flocks

People go to Africa and

South America to see many flamingos. In the United States, flamingos are popular zoo animals. It is fun to see these bright and colorful birds!

A flamingo often stands on one leg, sometimes while sleeping

A Flamingo Story

Why do flamingos like salty water? People in South America told a story about this. There once was a water goddess who watched over a special pond. The pond was for everyone to enjoy, but some men did not want to share. They fought the goddess's guards. The goddess was so sad that she cried and cried. Her tears became a salty lake. The guards turned into flamingos who have lived there ever since.

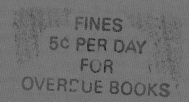
Read More

Malone, Jean M. *Flamingos*. New York: Grosset & Dunlap, 2009.

Pingry, Patricia A. *Baby Flamingo*. Nashville: CandyCane Press, 2004.

Websites

Enchanted Learning: Flamingo
http://www.enchantedlearning.com/subjects/birds/label/flamingo/
This site has facts about the flamingo and a picture to label and color.

San Diego Zoo Kids: Caribbean Flamingo
http://kids.sandiegozoo.org/animals/birds/caribbean-flamingo
Learn about Caribbean flamingos and watch a video of flamingos
at the zoo.

Note: Every effort has been made to ensure that the websites listed above are suitable for children, that they have educational value, and that they contain no inappropriate material. However, because of the nature of the Internet, it is impossible to guarantee that these sites will remain active indefinitely or that their contents will not be altered.

Index